History In Our Attics:

Photos and Documents of Brunswick, Maryland

James R. Castle

Volume II

Published by James R. Castle

October 2015

History In Our Attics:
Photos and Documents of Brunswick, Maryland.
Volume II

James R. Castle
P.O. Box 8
Brunswick, MD 21716

www.Jamesrcastle.com
www.facebook.com/authorjamesrcastle
Follow me on Twitter @Jamesrcastle
Email:Jamesrcastle@comcast.net

Dedication

To you, dear reader, for making this project worthwhile.

To my entire family and specifically my nephew Willie Ahalt and my sister Jennifer Ahalt for their help and support.

To my wife Monica, whom I love wholeheartedly, now, and forever.

Acknowledgments

This book is not meant to be a "history" of Brunswick. There are other books that serve that purpose. The purpose of this book is to highlight items in the author's personal collection and share his knowledge of those items. The items pictured are not representative of the author's "best" items and future volumes will highlight more from the collection.

Thanks to you, readers, who wish to remember the good times and/or read about those good times.

Thanks to my brother-in-law, Billy Ahalt, for letting me borrow some of his fire collection.

Special thanks to Alex Matsuo for her editing skills.

Special thanks to my father, James E. Castle, for discussing railroad logistics and staring at countless photos every day I worked on this book.

Thank you America, where I am allowed to write what I want and able to self-publish, just like Franklin.

About the Author
James R. Castle

James R. Castle was born and raised in the Brunswick/Knoxville area of Frederick County, Maryland. Instead of television or radio, James entertained and educated himself by listening to the stories of his family members and of the elders of his community. Weekends would find James looking for arrow points along a river or digging for bottles from old abandoned dump sites.

James currently resides in Brunswick, MD with his wife, Monica. In his limited free time, James is pursuing a degree from the University of Maryland. He also metal detects, researches, writes and investigates the paranormal. Known as a source on Brunswick area history, James conducts much research on families and properties in the area. He assists the local government with historical research and often contributes to a local weekly newspaper, The Brunswick Citizen. His first book, History In Our Attics: Photos and Documents of Brunswick, Maryland was published in 2014.

FOREWORD

More! That's what readers of Volume I told me they wanted. Readers wrote letters, sent emails, conversed with me and posted on social media. The response was unanimous: they all wanted "more".

"More" is the premise of Volume II. More railroad, more from the Brunswick YMCA, more Brunswick businesses, and more from the Brunswick Volunteer Fire Company.

A few new topics are being introduced in this volume; they are Gross' Store, Brunswick schools, and the Village of Knoxville.

I hope you enjoy this as much as I have enjoyed creating it. I'll keep writing as long as you keep reading and asking for "more" historical photos and documents of Brunswick, Maryland.

-James R. Castle

TABLE OF CONTENTS

Title Page   Page 1

Contact Page   Page 2

Dedication   Page 3

Acknowledgements   Page 4

About the Author   Page 5

Forward   Page 6

Table of Contents   Page 7

Chapter 1: More Brunswick Railroading   Page 8

Chapter 2: Brunswick Schools   Page 28

Chapter 3: Digital Restoration   Page 45

Chapter 4: More Brunswick Businesses   Page 48

Chapter 5: Preserving Brunswick's History Page 61

Chapter 6: William L. Gross' Store   Page 66

Chapter 7: Knoxville   Page 80

Chapter 8: More Fire Company   Page 92

Reader's Comments   Page 97

Suggested Reading   Page 98

Coming 2016   Page 99

Chapter One
More Brunswick Railroading

East End B. & O. Gravity Yards, Brunswick, Md.

When completed, the seven mile long rail yards at Brunswick were the longest owned by a single company[1]. This 1912 postcard was offered to folks who wanted to share what the East End B&O Gravity Rail Yard looked like. The postcard was published by L.S. Harmon who owned a cigar store on what is now West Potomac Street as well as serving as Brunswick's Mayor from 1902–1906.

[1] Brunswick History Commission, 100 Years of History, Page 48

This picture depicts two men standing in front of the Eastbound Station, which was located opposite of the current Westbound station, on the canal side of the tracks. As automobile travel increased, passenger travel by rail decreased and the building became underutilized and fell into disrepair. After the station was lost to a fire it was not replaced.

Not only did the railroad offer passenger service to Washington, DC but also to Hagerstown and Frederick, Maryland.

New Type of B. & O. Engine at Brunswick, Md.

B&O Engines in Brunswick

A new type of engine in Brunswick, circa 1910 was cause for this postcard, showing off engine 4013 and two railroad workers. This postcard was published by L.S. Harman and was available to be purchased in his tobacco and general goods store on what is now West Potomac Street. Luis Kaufman & Sons from Baltimore created these type of postcards for local businesses to sell featuring local views.

This photo shows B&O Engine 6154 in Brunswick during the 1930's. The engine is an S-1, 2-10-2 built by the Lima Locomotive works in Lima, Ohio in 1924. The engine was scrapped in 1953.

B&O Railroad engine 609, constructed in 1905, standing in Brunswick.

Five Brunswick men standing in front of B&O engine 2100. Notice the masonic symbol on the coal tender.

A class KB–1 Baldwin, which was built in 1934 and scrapped in 1953, standing in Brunswick.

More Brunswick YMCA

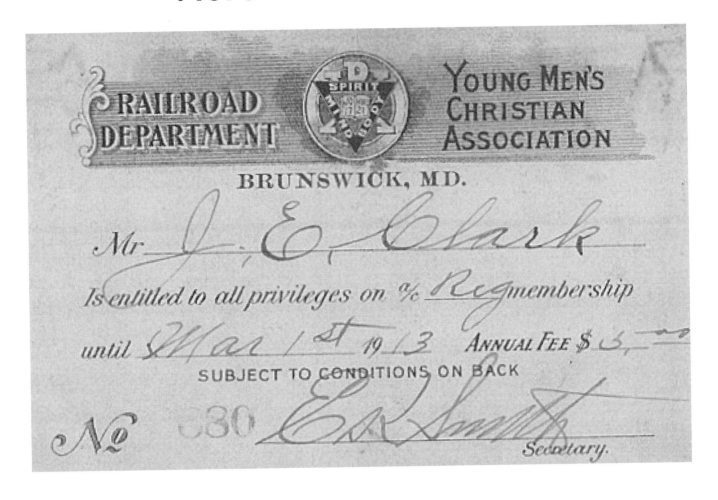

J.E. Clark paid $5.00 for his annual regular membership to the Brunswick YMCA, and was paid up until March 1, 1913. The membership card was signed by Brunswick YMCA Secretary E. Smith. The YMCA relied on selling memberships to offset operating costs.

Here, we see William "Bill" Dunn walking and talking with Evelyn Webber Darr. The Brunswick YMCA is in the background to the left and the Brunswick Roundhouse is to the right. Darr worked for the Brunswick YMCA and Bill Dunn spent a lot of time there. He knew more about the railroad then some of the bosses there. Bill memorized where railroad cars and cabooses were located in the yard and sometimes the yardmaster would call upon Dunn to help locate a missing car or caboose.

Victory Mail or V–Mail was a mail process used during World War II. A V–Mail letter would be censored, copied to film and then printed. This V–Mail message was from a member of the US Army, 82nd Airborne Division, sending Christmas greetings to the Brunswick YMCA in 1943.

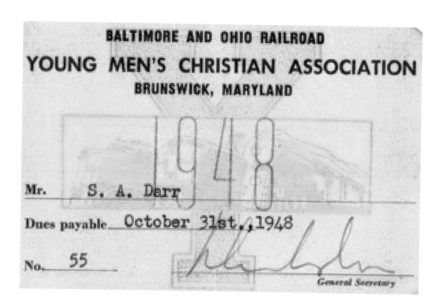

This 1948 Brunswick YMCA membership card belonged to Sam Darr.

Here are two sides to a Brunswick B&O YMCA towel check. A towel check was provided to a customer and traded for a towel. If the towel was not returned, the customer did not receive a towel check back. Simply put, no towel check meant no towel. This was a way to stop the theft of towels from the Brunswick "Y".

Brunswick YMCA Secretary, Marvin E. Younkins, welcomes a railroader to the Brunswick YMCA in the early 1950's. This picture was created for a public relations campaign to encourage railroaders to join the Brunswick YMCA.

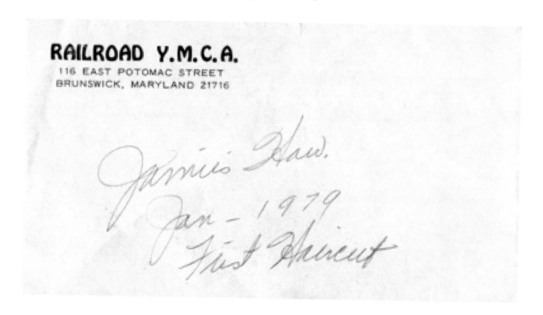

National War Fund in Maryland, Inc., acknowledges with grateful appreciation the gift of

Evelyn Webber

Cash Herewith One days wages

Balance

Date 10/10/44   Signed B&O YMCA

Solicitor

TEMPORARY RECEIPT

This receipt shows Evelyn Webber Darr offering one day's worth of wages to the war fund in 1944.

RAILROAD Y.M.C.A.
116 EAST POTOMAC STREET
BRUNSWICK, MARYLAND 21716

James Haw.
Jan - 1979
First Haircut

The author's first haircut was provided at the Brunswick B&O YMCA in January of 1979. At that time the railroad barber was Ken Harshman, who barbered at the YMCA until it burned in 1980 and then moved to the Feete building.

Taken from the WB Tower, this view shows the first Brunswick Roundhouse that was built in 1891. The building was demolished for a new roundhouse in 1907.

This photograph shows the Eastbound Hump Tower, located in receiving and classification yard. Workers in this tower directed the switching of cars to be reclassified for their new Eastbound destination.

This photograph shows a young Brunswick area porter. A porter is a railway employee who assists passengers aboard a passenger train and handles their baggage. Prior to the 1960's most all porters were African American men. It was not uncommon for some porters to be young men under 18 years old.

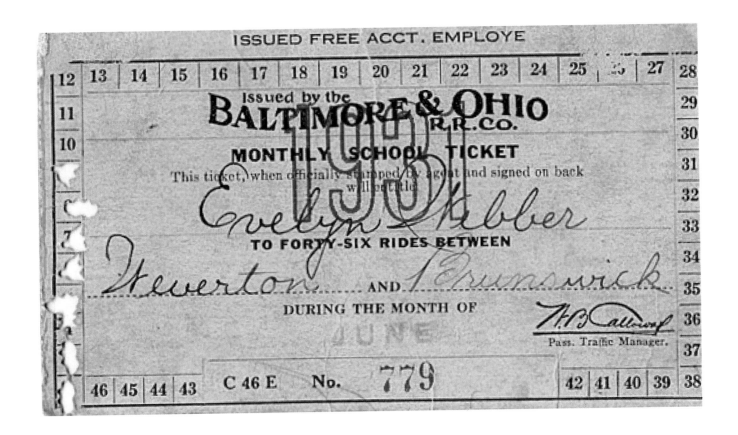

B&O Railroad employees had many perks that came with the job, including free passes to travel via the railroad. Evelyn Webber Darr received this pass to travel 46 times between Weverton and Brunswick to attend school in 1931. The pass is mostly unused because school ended on June 9th. She received this pass because her father, Robert A. Webber (who is also the author's great-grandfather), was a B&O railroad employee.

More Union

Union ribbons were issued by the various railroad trade unions and worn for various occasions. The black side was worn for funerals and the colorful side was worn for parades and conventions.

Union Advertisement from a 1950's railroad Trade Magazine

THE PUBLIC IS CORDIALLY INVITED TO ATTEND THE

Third Annual

PICNIC

Brotherhood of Maintenance of Way Employes

Rocky Mountain Lodge No. 993

Brunswick City Park **Brunswick, Md.**

4 P.M. TO 12 P.M.

Saturday, Aug. 28

AMUSEMENTS · · SPEAKING

ENTERTAINMENT AND MUSIC BY
THE SADDLE PALS FROM RADIO STATION WJEJ
HAGERSTOWN, MARYLAND

REFRESHMENTS OF ALL KINDS FOR SALE

All proceeds from the Picnic will be used to buy
WAR BONDS

COME AND BRING YOUR FRIENDS

This World War II era poster advertised a union picnic to be held a Brunswick City Park. All proceeds would be used to buy war bonds.

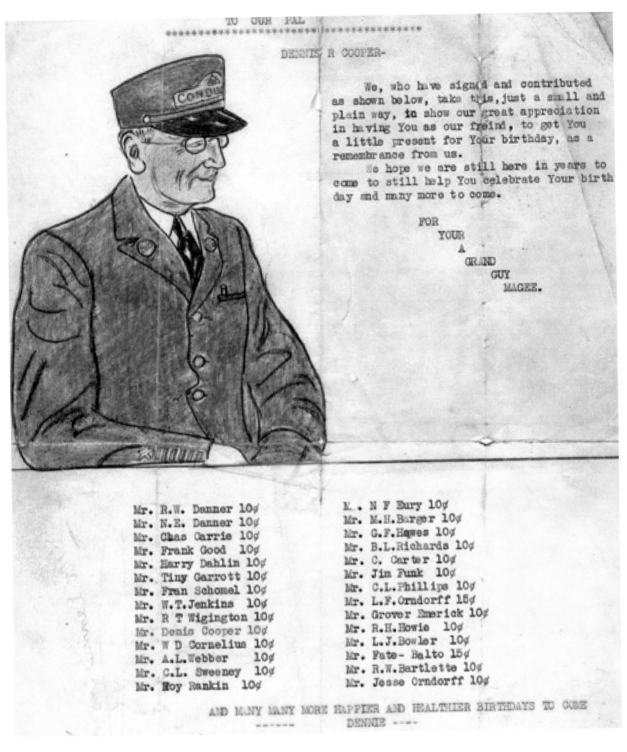

Paying into the birthday fund was a common tradition on the railroad. This paper shows 28 railroad workers chipping in for a birthday gift for Dennis R. Cooper, who was a conductor on the B&O Railroad.

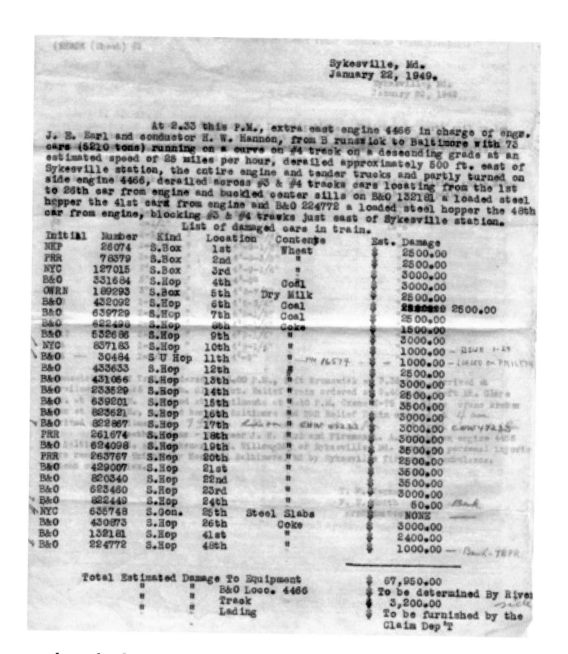

Sykesville, Md.
January 22, 1949.

At 2.33 this P.M., extra east engine 4466 in charge of engr. J. B. Earl and conductor H. W. Hannon, from B runswick to Baltimore with 73 cars (5210 tons) running on a curve on #4 track on a descending grade at an estimated speed of 25 miles per hour, derailed approximately 500 ft. east of Sykesville station, the entire engine and tender trucks and partly turned on side engine 4466, derailed across #3 & #4 tracks cars locating from the 1st to 26th car from engine and buckled center sills on B&O 132181 a loaded steel hopper the 41st car from engine and B&O 224772 a loaded steel hopper the 48th car from engine, blocking #3 & #4 tracks just east of Sykesville station.

List of damaged cars in train.

Initial	Number	Kind	Location	Contents	Est. Damage
NKP	26074	S.Box	1st	Wheat	$ 2500.00
PRR	78379	S.Box	2nd	"	$ 2500.00
NYC	127015	S.Box	3rd	"	$ 3000.00
B&O	331684	S.Hop	4th	Coal	$ 3000.00
OWRN	189293	S.Box	5th	Dry Milk	$ 2500.00
B&O	432092	S.Hop	6th	Coal	$ 2500.00
B&O	639729	S.Hop	7th	Coal	$ 2500.00
B&O	622498	S.Hop	8th	Coke	$ 1500.00
B&O	532686	S.Hop	9th	"	$ 3000.00
NYC	837183	S.Hop	10th	"	$ 1000.00
B&O	30484	S U Hop	11th	"	$ 1000.00
B&O	433633	S.Hop	12th	"	$ 2500.00
B&O	431066	S.Hop	13th	"	$ 3000.00
B&O	233529	S.Hop	14th	"	$ 2500.00
B&O	639201	S.Hop	15th	"	$ 3500.00
B&O	823621	S.Hop	16th	"	$ 3000.00
B&O	622867	S.Hop	17th	"	$ 3000.00
PRR	261674	S.Hop	18th	"	$ 3000.00
B&O	624098	S.Hop	19th	"	$ 3500.00
PRR	263767	S.Hop	20th	"	$ 2500.00
B&O	429007	S.Hop	21st	"	$ 3500.00
B&O	820340	S.Hop	22nd	"	$ 3500.00
B&O	623480	S.Hop	23rd	"	$ 3000.00
B&O	822449	S.Hop	24th	"	$ 50.00
NYC	635748	S.Gon.	25th	Steel Slabs	NONE
B&O	430873	S.Hop	26th	Coke	$ 3000.00
B&O	132181	S.Hop	41st	"	$ 2400.00
B&O	224772	S.Hop	48th	"	$ 1000.00

Total Estimated Damage To Equipment $ 67,950.00
     "   "   B&O Loco. 4466 $ To be determined By River
     "   "   Track $ 3,200.00
     "   "   Lading $ To be furnished by the Claim Dep't

Not only did train wrecks create a mess on the tracks, but they also generated much paperwork. This is merely the first page of a ten page document detailing a freight train derailment in Sykesville, Maryland on January 22, 1949. Note the monetary total of the loss, not including the engine, to be $67,950.

Smoke Town

Seeing smoke over Brunswick was not uncommon. These photos shows various railroad buildings and trains producing smoke and the nickname "Smoke Town" stuck. The nickname is still used to this day.

Chapter Two
Brunswick Schools
Educating Our Youth

Much is left to the imagination when it comes to the education of our earliest settlers. Written documents concerning this subject are non-existent until the 1830's. It was common practice to educate children within the home while also teaching them important life skills such as cleaning, sewing, hunting, fishing and cooking.

In 1838, Berlin was school district number 16 of 81 districts. From 1840 until 1847 an average of $90.00 per year was collected and distributed in the Berlin district. Enrollment averaged about 100 students. The location of this school house was or teachers requires more research.[2]

The first known school house was located on what is now the corner of Maple Avenue and West B Street. Made of logs, it was replaced in 1869 and used as a one room school until 1890. Later the property became an education annex for the First Baptist Church. Today, it is a private residence.

[2] Brunswick History Commission, 100 Years of Memories, Page 82

West End Public School Building, Brunswick, Md.

In 1890, W.W. Wenner donated an acre of land on Brunswick Street for a one room schoolhouse. This schoolhouse was later moved to J Street to be used as a school for Brunswick's African-American children. The County built another school and added rooms on the Brunswick Street Property. The School would be known as the West Brunswick School. As a general rule, if a child lived West of Maple Avenue, that child attended West Brunswick School. Today, the building houses the Masonic Lodge and the VFW. One side was used as the Public Library until the late 1980's.

In 1892, the B&O Railroad donated two acres of land at what is now Sixth Avenue and A Street. By 1901 it served 374 students, and in 1902, 4 more rooms were added to accommodate the growing population for Brunswick High School. When Brunswick High School was built in 1913 at the top of Fourth Avenue, this building was solely used as East Brunswick Elementary School. As a general rule, if a child lived East of Maple Avenue, that child attended East Brunswick School. Today, the structure is now an apartment building.

Brunswick Children
Learning and At Play

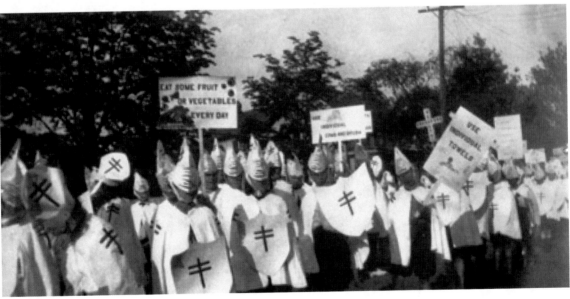

Brunswick school children dressed as "Health Crusaders" showing Brunswick veterans what they learned about hygiene.

West Brunswick school children lined up to parade dressed as fruit and vegetables.

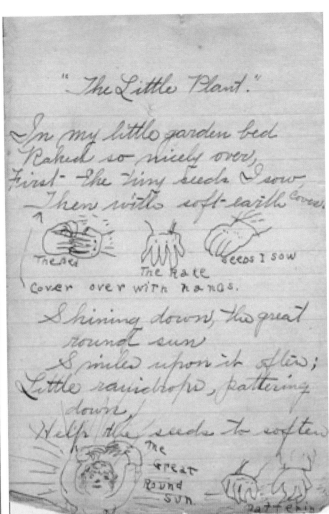

These three images shows Grace Mills' notebook used at West Brunswick School. The notebook was provided or purchased from Hovermale's Pharmacy which was located across from the old fire hall on West Potomac Street.

School photos show us contrasting economic conditions. The photo on the top shows a Brunswick class photo during the depression. Notice the homemade clothing and some sad faces. The bottom photo shows a Brunswick class photo from the 1950's. In this picture we notice some happier children and stylish clothing.

Another class photo.

Three young men eating lunch on the playground.

New Brunswick Elementary School

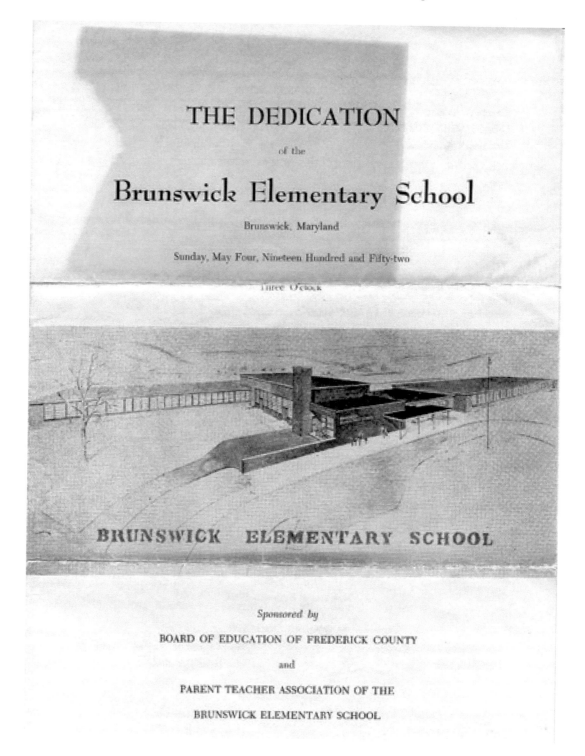

THE DEDICATION

of the

Brunswick Elementary School

Brunswick, Maryland

Sunday, May Four, Nineteen Hundred and Fifty-two

Three O'clock

BRUNSWICK ELEMENTARY SCHOOL

Sponsored by

BOARD OF EDUCATION OF FREDERICK COUNTY

and

PARENT TEACHER ASSOCIATION OF THE

BRUNSWICK ELEMENTARY SCHOOL

The current Brunswick Elementary School was constructed in 1952. Students from West End and East End converged into one school.

PROGRAM

ORGAN RECITAL .... Donald Darr

SONG: *America The Beautiful* .... Assembly

INVOCATION .... Reverend George W. Bennett,
Pastor, First Methodist Church

WELCOME .... T. Woodrow Souder

INTRODUCTIONS .... Mr. Rhoderick, President
Frederick County Board of Education

ARCHITECTS: Paul H. Kea Associates .... Represented by Paul H. Kea

CONTRACTORS: A. R. Warner and Son
Presentation of Keys

DEDICATION:

George C. Rhoderick, Jr. .... President of Board of Education
Eugene W. Pruitt .... Superintendent of Frederick County Schools
Dr. Thomas G. Pullen, Jr. .... State Superintendent of Schools
U. Grant Hooper .... President, County Commissioners
E. Virginia Weaver .... Principal, Brunswick Elementary School
Herman A. Hauver .... Principal, Brunswick High School

Pupils

Shirley Lloyd .... Sixth Grade
Richard Nichols .... Sixth Grade

BENEDICTION .... Reverend Leonard Carrack,
Pastor, First Baptist Church

Tour of Building

Social Hour – Multi-Purpose Room

BOARD OF EDUCATION

George C. Rhoderick, Jr., *President*	Mrs. John N. Howie
George J. Martin, *Vice President*	Claude U. Shetlecuyer
Mrs. Kent C. Nicodemus	Joseph F. Rhoderick

Eugene W. Pruitt, *Secretary-Treasurer*

BOARD OF COUNTY COMMISSIONERS

U. Grant Hooper, *President*

Robert R. Rhoderick	Samuel H. Young

PARENT TEACHER ASSOCIATION

T. Woodrow Souder, *President*	Mrs. A. Dan Arnold, *Secretary*
Mrs. James S. Cise, 1st Vice *President*	Mrs. Ralph N. Manuel, *Treasurer*
Mrs. John R. Goodrich, 2nd Vice *President*	

FACULTY OF THE BRUNSWICK ELEMENTARY SCHOOL

E. Virginia Weaver, *Principal*
Mrs. Virginia L. Bush
Peggy Ann Carter
Mrs. Hazel N. Goode
Margaret L. Hatcher
Georgia A. Hood
M. Lavonia Hood
Jacqueline Keller
Mrs. Eva F. Magalis
Katherine B. Mason
Mrs. Frances N. Manuel
Mrs. Ottie E. Miller
Mrs. Julia D. Stine
Mrs. Margaret H. Strullman
Stanley M. Swish
Elsie L. Talbott
Mrs. Louise F. Grams, *Clerk*

SCHOOL LUNCHROOM

Mrs. Frances Chew, *Co-manager*	Mrs. Virginia M. Nichols, *Co-manager*
Mrs. Ruth Best	Mrs. Helen Cornelius

CUSTODIANS

Raymond A. Castro	George W. Mourn, Jr.
Mrs. Agnes J. Walker	Harry Catlett

These four images are from the dedication booklet of the new Brunswick Elementary School in 1952.

PLATFORM GUESTS

State Senator Jacob R. Ramsburg

Members of the House of Delegates:
Horace M. Alexander
Melvin H. Derr
S. Fenton Harris
Joseph B. Payne
C. Clifton Virts

Former members of Board of Education:
Harry Y. George
Charles S. Lane, III
Dr. Paul B. Kallaway

Former principal of Brunswick School
Ella V. Krieg
Mrs. Anna Nichols, Former Teacher

State Department of Education
Dr. R. Floyd Cromwell
Dr. John J. Seidel
Dr. James E. Spitznas
Miss Eleanor Weagly
Dr. David W. Zimmerman

Dr. Wilbur Devilbiss, Dean of Education, University of Maryland

D. C. Turnbull, Executive Assistant to
President of Baltimore and Ohio Railroad

H. E. Bodie, Terminal Trainmaster of the
Baltimore and Ohio Railroad

B. Lee Foote, President
Frederick County Parent Teacher Association Council

City of Brunswick:
Stanley T. Virts, Mayor
John B. Funk, Engineer
W. Claude Latman, Clerk
Forest G. Moler, Finance Commission Chairman
Frank J. Supp, President, Board of Trade

This building was begun in December 1950. Total cost, including architets' fees, furniture, and other equipment, was $470,805.00. It contains sixteen classrooms, a multi-purpose room, library and administrative and health rooms and is situated upon a landscaped playground of 24.63 cres, purchased from the Fraternal Order of Eagles at a cost of $5,319.00.

The dedication program listed all the staff and the program was very professional with music, speeches, tour, and a social hour.

Brunswick High School

High school students had it rough before the construction of Brunswick High in 1913. Prior to 1900, students rode a train to Frederick or Hagerstown to attend this level of education. The first high school building was located at the corner of East Potomac Street and 6th Avenue, called the Westall House. In 1905 the four room addition to East Brunswick was used for high school students. In 1904 a law was passed requiring all children between eight and 12 to attend public school. Overcrowding again became a problem. Eventually churches were used and building were rented to house school students. Finally in 1912, construction of a new high school in Brunswick started and in 1913, at a cost of $40,000. Students began attending Brunswick High School at the top of Fourth Avenue. [3]

The building suffered from a fire in February of 1928. Approximately $125,000 later, the fire damage was fixed and the school was enlarged and opened in September of 1928.

[3] Brunswick History Commission, 100 Years of Memories, Pages 84 & 85

High School, Brunswick, Md.

These two postcards show different views of Brunswick High School.

These "Senior Cards" were distributed amongst friends to offer a remembrance of them during their school life together.

FOURTH ANNUAL

Gymnastic Exhibition

—OF—

Brunswick High School Boys and Girls

FRIDAY, MARCH 15, 1935

7:30 P. M.

PROGRAM

MARCH	ALL CLASSES
FLORAL COTILLION	SENIOR GIRLS
MIMETIC DRILL	ALL GIRLS
HYMN TO THE SUN	JUNIOR GIRLS
BOYS' EVENTS	SEVENTH GRADE BOYS

MARCHING
CALISTHENICS
MONKEY ROLL
CAMEL RACE
TWO HIGH RACE
WHEEL BARROW RACE

SHAMROCK JIG	NINTH GRADE GIRLS
MORRIS DANCE	EIGHTH GRADE GIRLS
WAND DRILL	SEVENTH GRADE GIRLS
TAP DANCES	GIRLS
PYRAMID BUILDING	EIGHTH AND NINTH GRADE BOYS
ROPE CLIMBING	JUNIOR AND SENIOR BOYS
STUNTS	EIGHTH AND NINTH GRADE BOYS

HAND SPRINGS
SHOULDER BALANCE
PULL OVER THE LEG
HAND AND FOOT SWING
SKATE WHIRL

RELAYS	GIRLS

JUDGES' DECISION AND AWARDING OF THE PENNANT.

This small program is from the fourth annual gymnastic exhibition from 1935. The event must have been quite entertaining as it included marching, wheel barrow race, pyramid building, dancing, stunts, and relay racing. Everything back then seemed so organized!

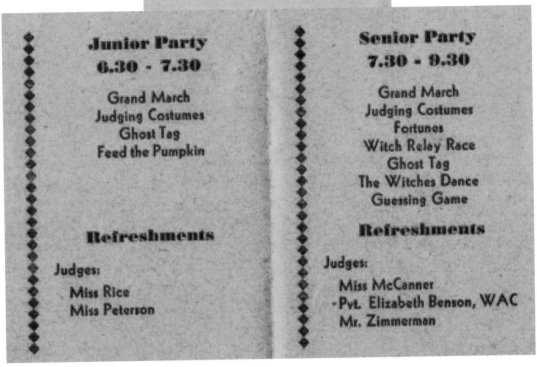

Junior Party
6.30 - 7.30

Grand March
Judging Costumes
Ghost Tag
Feed the Pumpkin

Refreshments

Judges:
Miss Rice
Miss Peterson

Senior Party
7.30 - 9.30

Grand March
Judging Costumes
Fortunes
Witch Relay Race
Ghost Tag
The Witches Dance
Guessing Game

Refreshments

Judges:
Miss McConner
Pvt. Elizabeth Benson, WAC
Mr. Zimmerman

This keepsake is from a Brunswick High School Junior/Senior Halloween party. Notice how the two classes did not interact and held parties a different times.

Senior Pep Song: (Tune to Margie)

I   You've heard tales about this senior class,

Some of them perhaps are true,

Stor-ies told about each lad and lass,

Heres' some that we will tell to you.

Chories:

Boys: We may be naught---y,

Girls: You can be sure were Nevery haught---y

All: In all your games we shout the laud-est for dear old B. H. S.

In our classes we all try to do our best. For Brunswick,

our dear old high school, with your days are all too few.

But all calsses must have fun. For us there is only one

Oh: nineteen forty, its you.

II   Boys: We've won many games for B. H. S.

Girls: In our cheers we've done our part.

All : We have worked to pass each lousy test,

Until we know the stuff by heart,

(Repeat choris)

This senior pep song was typed and distributed amongst the seniors and was to be sung during the graduation ceremony.

Chapter Three
Digital Restoration

Eastbound station before restoration.

Eastbound station after restoration

Gross' Store before restoration.

Gross' Store after restoration.

Heritage Photo Services

Archiving, Preserving, and Repairing photos for generations to come

Website: heritagephotoservices.photography/photo-restoration

Email: tina@hagerstownweddingphotographer.com

Chapter Four
More Brunswick Businesses

Most Popular Store in Brunswick. Md.

Pub. by J. E. Shilling, Brunswick, Md.

This postcard is dated from the early 1900's, and shows J.E. Shilling's General Merchandise store. The store was located across from the B&O Station. The postcard states that Shilling's was the most popular store in Brunswick. Ironically, the postcard was also published by J.E. Shilling.

This is a Hoyt's German Cologne Calendar, which was provided to the customers of C.N. Skiltneck who dealt in drugs, patent medicines, chemicals, fancy and toilet articles, brushes, perfumery, etc. The calendar is from 1899 and would have been given away during the Christmas season of 1898. The author has researched but has not gained any knowledge of the location of the store.

L.S. Harman's Cigar Store

THE HARMAN BUILDING, BRUNSWICK, MD.

Lewis S. Harman constructed the Harman building and operated his cigar shop in one of the storefronts. The other storefront was a general merchandise store. Harman was very involved within the Brunswick community and served as Mayor from 1902–1906. In addition to cigars, his store carried other items including postcards that he commissioned of Brunswick views. Today, the building is the current home of Head-Quarters Barber and Styling Salon.

This receipt shows W.L. Gross purchasing cigars for resale from L.S. Harman in 1896.

This envelope contained postcards depicting Brunswick views that Harman would offer for sale.

This wooden cigar box is from L.S. Harman's cigar store in Brunswick, MD.

In addition to printing the local newspaper "The Brunswick Herald", E.C. Shafer also was an insurance agent. This ink blotter shows him as an agent for The Home Insurance Company of New York.

Hardware

This receipt, dated 1904, is from Swank & George. The business started in 1893 as Wenner, Swank & Co. and was located on the South Side of the tracks of what is now South Virginia Avenue. In 1902 Wenner had sold out to the remaining partners, Swank and George. This receipt shows William Schnauffer, as agent for the B&O Real Estate Department, purchasing items for upkeep of railroad buildings.

The JERSEY
Ice Cream
FREEZER

THE BEST in practical use, because convenient, compact in size use smallest amount of ice and salt, run easily, freeze quickly, produce smoothly frozen creams or desserts with little bother and less work.

The **Pails have electric-welded wire hoops,** which are guaranteed not to break or fall off; the Cans are made of heavy tinplate with **drawn steel bottoms** that are guaranteed not to fall out or break and do not leak, the strongest and most durable Freezer Can made; the **Automatic Twin Scrapers** by their positive action insure perfect scraping of frozen particles from side of can as rapidly as formed without injury to Can or Scrapers. All inside parts are heavily coated with pure block tin, and outside parts all thoroughly galvanized. A Recipe Book with complete directions for making over 100 Ice Creams, Water Ices, Sherbets and other desserts tucked in each Freezer.

SAMUEL W. GEORGE & CO.   -   -   BRUNSWICK, MD.

Swank & George split and in 1907, and S.W.George constructed a new building on the corner of what is now West Potomac Street and Delaware Avenue. The building continues as a hardware store today. This trade card advertises The Jersey Ice Cream Freezer for sale at Samuel W. George & Co.

Two advertising match book covers. On the left, the Whistle Stop advertises that they offered food. The cover on the right is for Foster's Lunch Room, which was a food establishment that began offering beer right after the repeal of Prohibition in 1933.

"The Blade–Times" was Brunswick's weekly newspaper for over fifty years. They also offered printing services. This ad is from 1920.

Harry R. Mace operated this store on West Potomac Street where King's Restaurant is now located. This ad is from 1920 and the store operated until the early 1950's.

This ink blotter advertised Chase & Sandborn's Seal Brand Coffee available at E.P. Orrison's.

ORRISON'S

QUALITY STORE.

OYSTERS.

WHOLESALE AND RETAIL.

OPEN SEPT. 1.

A 1920 advertisement from Orrison's.

A 1920 advertisement. Notice A. Hemp, who was a dealer in fresh meats of all kinds. Hemp started his store in Brunswick before moving it to Jefferson where it is still in operation today.

STATEMENT.

Brunswick, Md., May 14 1902

Mr Michael Everheart

To C. H. FEETE & BRO., Dr.,

.... DEALERS IN ....

Furniture, House Furnishings, &c.

C.H. Feete & Brother made furniture, as well as ran the funeral home. The furniture was manufactured in a building that was torn down. Today, a grey apartment building now sits on the same lot and has a footbridge that crosses the creek to North Maryland Avenue.

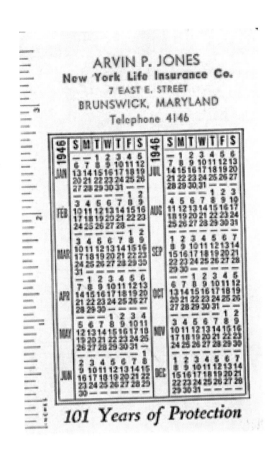

This is a 1946 pocket calendar from Arvin P. Jones who offered New York Life Insurance from his office on East Potomac Street.

Many a milk jug had this sticker placed on it from the ACME Market.

What Once Was, Could Be Again?

Potomac Street looking East
Brunswick, Md.

The Railroad Industry created a circular flow economy where money was earned, then spent, and reinvested back into the Town. The jobs paid well, and the stores provided all needed goods and services for the community. There was no need to travel to Frederick or Charlestown because all one needed was right here in Brunswick. West Potomac Street had parking on both sides of the street and was packed on Friday and Saturday nights. The sidewalks overflowed as people walked in the streets. The Dime Store made several deposits in one night. This is how it was. Now the question is, will it ever be again?

Chapter Five
Preserving Brunswick History

This photo, from the Brunswick Heritage Museum archives, shows the Berlin freight depot on the right. Notice the stone wall to the right of the railroad tracks.

In July of 2015, this hole was dug to prepare a foundation for the relocation of the WB Tower and a B&O Railroad caboose. The digging exposed walls and bricks from the old Berlin freight depot. This is a

close up photo of the remains of the same wall seen in the old Berlin freight depot photograph.

Local historian, Wade Watson looks for any remains of old Berlin.

The site of the old Berlin freight depot.

This photo, also from the Brunswick Heritage Museum archives, shows the Berlin Depot in the back left. Notice the decorative woodwork toward the top of the roof.

This photograph shows recovered decorative woodwork found in the old Berlin "pit" that matches the decorative woodwork seen in the above picture of the old Berlin freight depot.

Pictured **a**bove, the soil removed from the "Berlin Pit". Wade Watson removes our best find of the day from the soil. Our finds included a bench leg, ketchup bottle, and a whisky flask. Heartbreakers included a broken Brunswick soda bottle, a porcelain sign, and a broken civil war era wine bottle.

The author poses with the day's finds.

The best find of the day was this pre–1890 B&O RR baggage tag.

Chapter Six
William L. Gross
Gross' General Merchandise

William Lynch Gross was born in Jefferson, Maryland to Charles and Elizabeth (Boteler) Gross on August 11, 1857. W.L. Gross farmed on the family land in Jefferson until 1877. At twenty years of age, Gross traveled to Berlin and purchased half interest in Lingam Boteler's (most likely his uncle) general store, renaming it Bottler and Gross. [4]

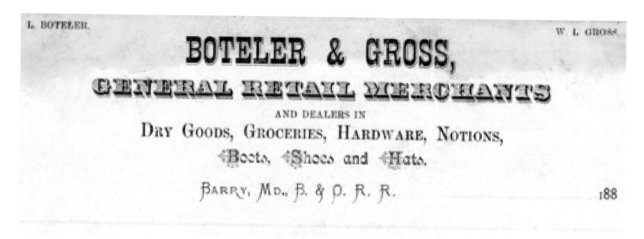

Boteler & Gross Lettehead from the 1880's.

Note that P.O. Box Barry, MD B&O RR was used instead of Berlin, MD. The store was located across the tracks in old Berlin near what is now South Virginia Avenue.

[4] T.J.C. Williams, History of Frederick County Maryland, Page 978

In 1886, Bottler wished to retire and W.L. Gross purchased the remaining interest from him. In the first year of operation, Berlin's population was around 300 people and the store conducted $10,000 in business transactions.[5]

This field sign is over seven feet long. It states" This field of corn was planted with a Deere and Mansur Co. Check Rower Planter, Manufactured at Moline, Ill. Sold by W. L. Gross, Berlin, MD".

The sign is the only known wooden sign to exist from Berlin and would have been placed in a local cornfield to advertise the implement and Gross' Store. Gross benefited greatly from being located near the B&O Railroad and this fact allowed him to pre-sale large items that could be delivered by train, quite literally, right to his door.

5 Ibid

W. L. Gross purchased land from Sarah Birmingham at what is now the bottom of South Maryland Avenue, and built a store in 1893. The building also housed a drug store and a dentist. The building had an elevator that operated by a rope pulley system.

Everyone wanted to be in the above picture shortly after the new store was constructed. The only names on the reverse are "Adam Wrench, Bud Ferrell, Hammond Gross, Grandma Gross, Lizzy Jennings, and father."

Three receipts from the 1890's.

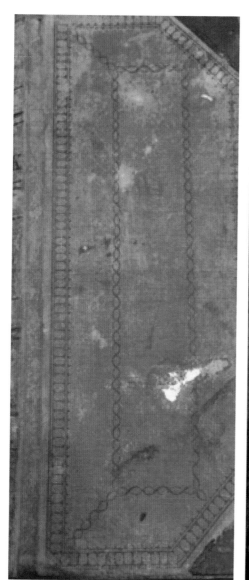
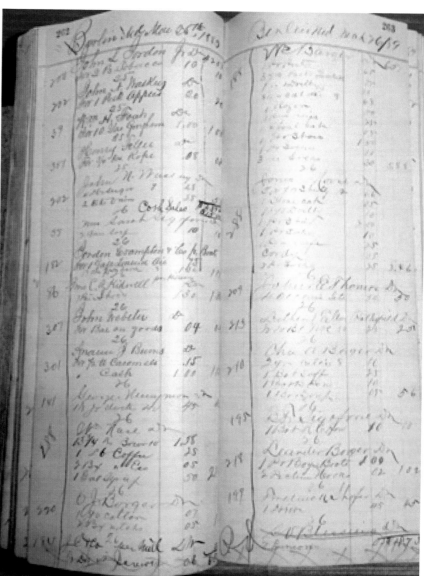

This ledger book from 1889–1890 contains the daily activities from Gross's Store. Cash sales were totaled but only credit customers were listed on the pages of the ledger.

This ink blotter advertises Morton's Salt that could be purchased from Wm. L. Gross, General Merchandise.

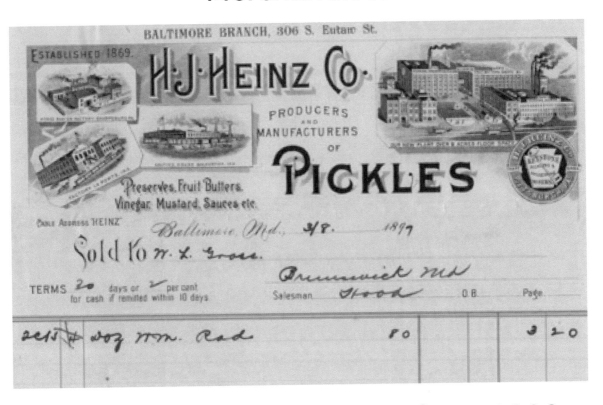

H. J. Heinz Pickles Bill head from 1899.

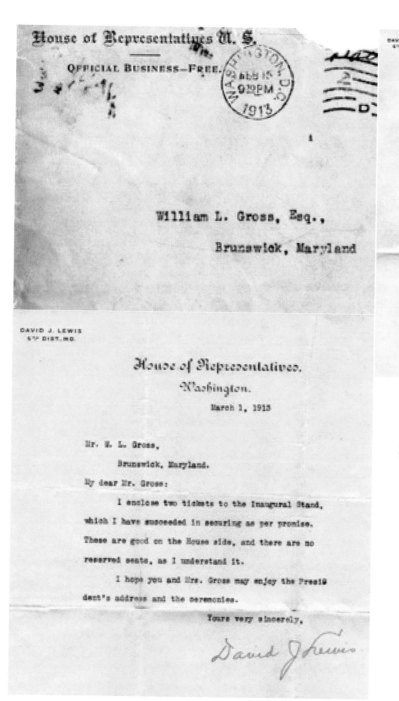

House of Representatives U. S.

OFFICIAL BUSINESS—FREE.

William L. Gross, Esq.,

Brunswick, Maryland

DAVID J. LEWIS
6TH DIST. MD.

House of Representatives.
Washington.

March 1, 1913

Mr. W. L. Gross,

Brunswick, Maryland.

My dear Mr. Gross:

I enclose two tickets to the Inaugural Stand, which I have succeeded in securing as per promise. These are good on the House side, and there are no reserved seats, as I understand it.

I hope you and Mrs. Gross may enjoy the President's address and the ceremonies.

Yours very sincerely,

David J Lewis

DAVID J. LEWIS
6TH DIST. MD.

House of Representatives U. S.
Washington, D. C.

Feb. 15, 1913

William L. Gross, Esq.,

Brunswick, Maryland

My dear Mr. Gross:

I have just ascertained what I am to be allotted in tickets to the east platform on Inauguration Day, and will be able to get you the two tickets. These are all the tickets I can secure, I am sorry to say, so that it will be impossible to get seats for any other friends.

I will mail you the tickets when they are distributed, so you will not have any trouble in getting to the platform.

With best wishes, I am

Yours very sincerely,

David J Lewis

Mr. Gross was an active citizen and a stanch adherent democrat. He once ran for the first Town Council in 1890 but lost and never sought political office again. The three items above are correspondence from Congressman David J. Lewis, who was able to attain tickets for Gross to attend the swearing in ceremony of President Woodrow Wilson.

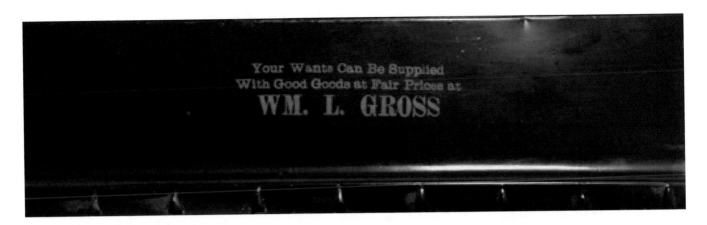

This picture shows a W. L. Gross display item, most likely it held seed packets.

A W. L. Gross envelope. In 1908, Gross' store sold $61,000 in merchandise which is comparable to about $1.5 million in todays economy.

WILLIAM L. GROSS

ALWAYS READY TO SERVE YOU.

GLAD OF YOUR PATRONAGE.

ESTABLISHED 1877.

An advertisement for W. L. Gross from 1920.

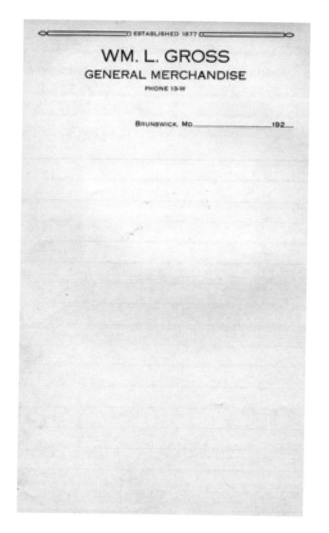

A notepad from the 1920's.

This calendar plate is from 1920 and is a tribute to the Great War, World War I. The plate says, "Victory" and has the flags from the coalition against Germany. The plate, most likely, was given away to customers as a premium or gift during the Christmas season of 1919.

WILLIAM L. GROSS

MEMBER FROM MARYLAND FOR 1914

BRUNSWICK, MARYLAND

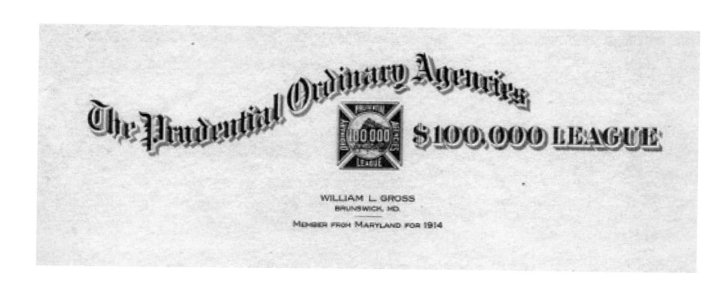

At some point in the middle of his career, William L. Gross engaged in the lucrative business of selling insurance. Above is his insurance business card and letterhead.

W. L. Gross was so successful in the insurance business he often earned trips as a reward. Notices of his awards were placed in the local weekly newspaper, The Brunswick Herald. Above, is a picture from one such trip. He loved to travel and that love was passed down to his children who also traveled often. Notice the car and the style of dress upon the ladies. Also notice the attire of the driver and the set of lights near the window. Looks like the Gross' took a trip to the North during the Fall season.

Two receipt books circa 1930's. One is from Prudential Life Insurance and the other is from the General Merchandise Store.

William L. Gross died on April 10, 1930. His body laid in repose in the front window of his store and the residents of Brunswick lined up Maryland Avenue to pass by to pay their respects. The general merchandise business ended. The building was used by his sons as Gross Brothers for a while.

An auction was held to sell the remains items left in the store, some, still in the box from when the store was located in old Berlin. The building remained vacant for many years and was lost to a fire in the late 1990's. The City of Brunswick acquired the lot and it is currently used a place for visitors to watch trains pass.

Chapter Seven

Knoxville

In 1732, British Captain James Knox camped at a spring before crossing the Potomac River, because the river was too high to safely cross. Knox traveled this same way several other times, earning the area to be later called Knoxville.[6]

The area know known as Knoxville was part of the "Merryland Tract" deeded to John Hawkins. It was first called Payne's delight after land owner Layle Payne and the creek that ran through it was called Payne's Creek.[7]

A settlement emerged and a ferry and grist mill went into operation there. The close proximity of Knoxville to the new B&O Railroad and the C&O Canal in the 1830's guaranteed growth and plans for industry.

The town grew and homes, businesses and churches were erected in Knoxville.

---

[6] H. Austin Cooper, The Church in the Valley, Page 515

[7] Life in A Small Town, 1880–1899:A Portrait of Knoxville, Maryland, Peter Maynard and Eleanor Milligan, Page 3

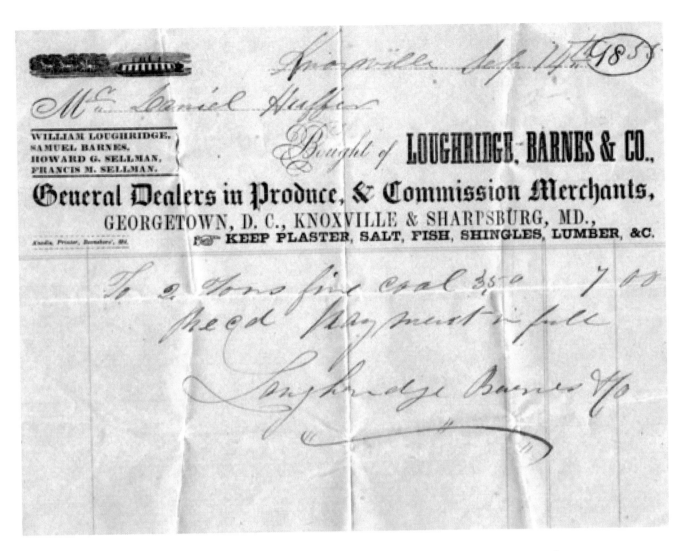

The close proximity of the C&O Canal was an economic asset for the village of Knoxville. This receipt is from 1855 and shows Daniel Huffer purchasing 2 tons of coal for $7.00 from Loughridge, Barnes & Co. The company dealt in produce and were merchants, selling other peoples goods for a commission. They were located in Georgetown, D.C., Knoxville & Sharpsburg, MD. What did these locations have in common? Close proximity to the C&O Canal.

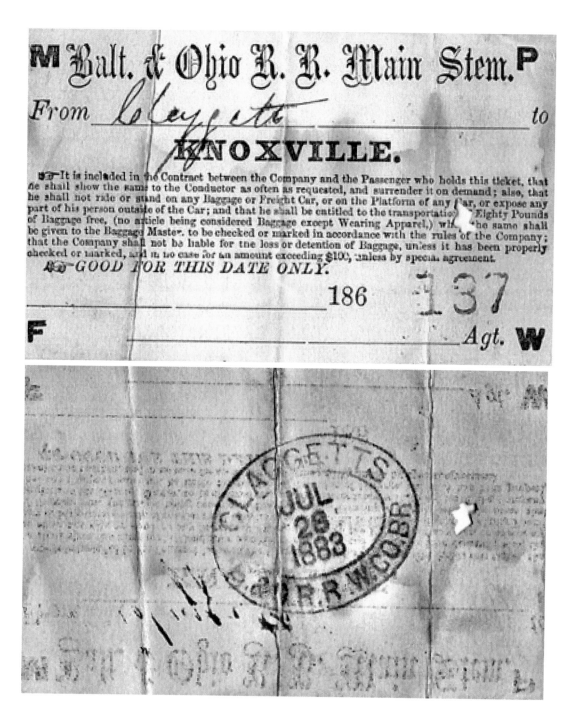

The B&O Railroad was an important mode of transportation for those who lived in Knoxville. This B&O ticket is dated from the 1860's. However it was not used until July 28, 1883. The passenger traveled to Claggetts, which is a stop on the B&O's Washington County Branch.

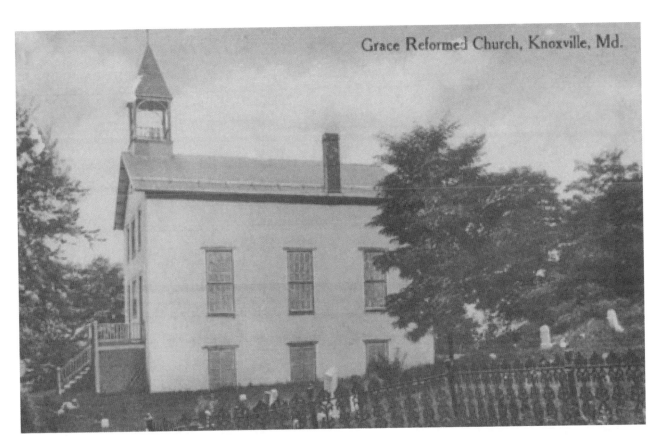
Grace Reformed Church, Knoxville, Md.

This postcard shows the Grace Reformed Church in Knoxville, MD. The church, which is located on Cemetery Circle, was started by German immigrants migrating from Holland. Construction on the church began in 1845. The church was used as a hospital by the Union Army after the battle of Antietam. The congregation tried to receive compensation from the federal government for damage sustained to church while under occupation. But the attempt proved futile as such claims from all over the country would have bankrupted the federal government. The property is now a private residence.

Post Office & R. F. D. Carrier, Knoxville, Md.

This real picture postcard shows one of the oldest houses in Knoxville at the corner of Cemetery Circle and Jefferson Pike. The structure is at least 225 years old and was built by Will Cooper. Cooper was a builder and some of the earliest homes Knoxville was built by him. The postcard was postmarked Knoxville, July 28, 1913 at 10:00 AM. The mail buggy traveled to Brunswick often as well as delivered mail to the surrounding rural area. How many people do you see in the photo? If you see less than seven, keep looking.

AS BLUE AS INDIGO and as fast is the fast, rich color made by the Diamond Indigo Blue Dye.

AS BLACK AS NIGHT are the Diamond Black Dyes. Black for Wool, Stocking Black for Cotton.

AS BROWN AS A NUT are the rich, deep colors made by the Diamond Fast Brown, Fast Seal Brown, and Fast Dark Brown Dyes.

AS BRIGHT AS SUNSET HUES are the fast and brilliant colors made by the Diamond Orange, Scarlet, Cardinal, and Crimson Dyes.

AS BEAUTIFUL AS RAINBOW TINTS are the brilliant colors made by Diamond Yellow, Light Blue, Green, Purple, and Violet Dyes.

AS RICH AS THOUGH FROM PERSIAN LOOMS are the shades made by the Diamond Dark Blue, Dark Green, Dark Wine, and Garnet Dyes.

AS RELIABLE AS GOLD are all the 37 tried and true colors made by Diamond Dyes.

Warranted to color more goods than any other dyes ever made. Ask for the Diamond and take no other.

For Gilding or Bronzing Fancy Articles Use Diamond Paints, Gold, Silver, Bronze, Copper, Artist's Black. Only 10 cents.

With compliments of

J. M. Miller, Merchant

Knoxville, Md.

Jobe M. Miller was born in 1839. His father owned a general store in Knoxville called Miller & Garrott. In 1870, J. M. Miller bought out his father and became the sole proprietor until he sold his business to his son, Daniel Miller in 1899. This colorful trade card advertises Diamond Dyes and was provided with compliments of J. M. Miller, Knoxville, Maryland.[8]

Miller served in the Maryland House of Delegates from 1873–1875.

---

[8] Ibid, Page 10

This box, circa 1880, contained fine stationary from the store of J.M. Miller, Knoxville, MD.

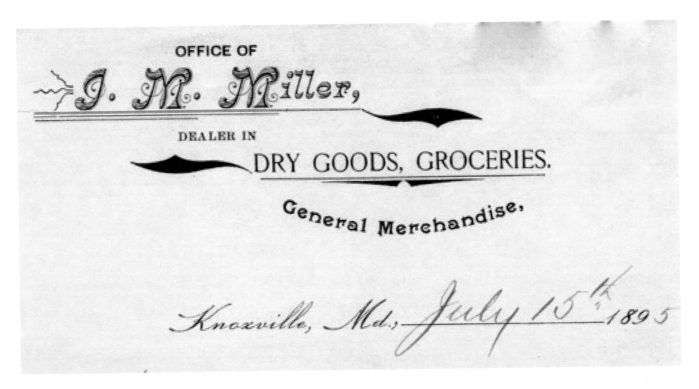

This bill head is from the office of J. M. Miller, Dealer in dry goods, groceries and general merchandise, Knoxville, MD. This particular note paper is dated July 15th, 1895.

The note under the letterhead requested Miller's attorney to file a judgement against one of his customers for placing items on account (credit) and not making any payments towards the balance for over a year. The note is purposely left out of the image to protect the identity of the accused, even if the accusations are from 1895.

HOTEL LEOPOLD,

J. W. LEOPOLD, Proprietor,

The Popular Resort for Fishermen,

KNOXVILLE, MARYLAND.

Boats For Hire by the Day and River Guides Furnished
When Desired at Reasonable Rates.

FINE, UP-TO-DATE BAR ATTACHED,

Containing the Choicest Wines, Liquors, Standard and Export
Beers and Soft Drinks of All Kinds   Also Sandwiches.

This is an advertising card from Hotel Leopold. The hotel was operated by J. W. Leopold. Billed as "The popular resort for fisherman". Why? The hotel offered boats for hire and a "fine, up-to-date bar that offered the choicest wines, liquors, beers and soft drinks of all kinds. You could also grab a sandwich. Oddly, the card does not address rooms for the hotel.

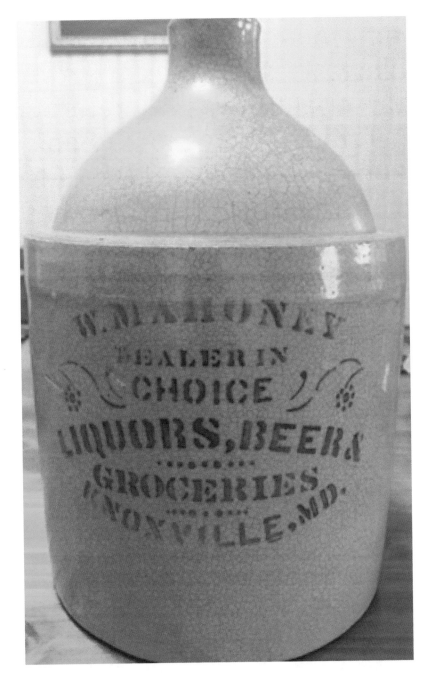

A December 9, 1898, advertisement in The Brunswick Herald stated, "Want a case of export or something good for the jug at Christmas, send your order to Wm. Mahoney, Knoxville." Pictured above is a blue painted stoneware jug advertising W. Mahoney, Dealer in Choice Liquors, Beer & Groceries, Knoxville, MD.

C. Frank Willard owned and operated the Knoxville Hotel, also called the Willard Hotel. He began operating the hotel in 1891. Willard also operated a livery stable behind the hotel. In the August 2, 1895 edition of the Brunswick Herald, it stated, "C.F. Willard has fitted up a beer bottling business in Knoxville, and this week will bottle Moerleins Cincinnati beer." The hotel soon became the site of many social activities. Many lavish meals and dances.

These are two examples of beer bottles from C.F. Willard, Knoxville, MD.

Knoxville area merchants could not keep up with the building boom in Brunswick. Soon, Brunswick stores and industrial jobs lured Knoxville residents to make the two mile trek into Brunswick for needed goods and to work on the railroad. The stores eventually closed and the village of Knoxville has remained, for the most part, a residential village.

Knoxville in a Broader Sense

Knoxville is more than just a tiny village, the Knoxville designation is also used in Petersville, on Route 340 West heading toward Charlestown, WVA, and also in Washington County.

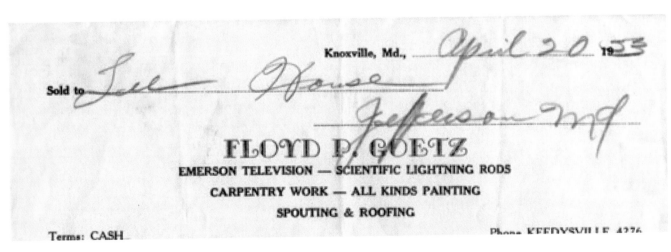

This 1953 receipt is from Floyd Goetz of Knoxville, MD to Lee House of Jefferson, MD. Notice the Keedysville phone exchange.

Chapter Eight
More Brunswick Volunteer Fire Company

This photograph, taken on July 13, 1931, shows Brunswick fireman Conner at the annual Maryland fireman's convention in Ocean City.

This is an honorary membership certificate received upon paying $3.00 to The Brunswick Volunteer Fire Company.

This is an unused membership certificate from the 1930's for the Brunswick Volunteer Fire Company.

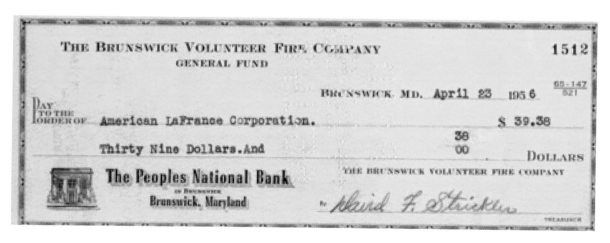

THE BRUNSWICK VOLUNTEER FIRE COMPANY
GENERAL FUND

Brunswick, Md., Jan 31 1956 No. 1443

PAY TO THE ORDER OF W S Rice. $52.94

Fifty Two. And 94/00   DOLLARS

THE PEOPLES NATIONAL BANK
IN BRUNSWICK
BRUNSWICK, MD.

THE BRUNSWICK VOLUNTEER FIRE COMPANY

by David F. Stickles
TREASURER

65-147
521

This is a check from 1956 to W.S. Rice for $52.94. Walter Rice was the first paid driver/engineer for the company in the 1950's. He lived in the firehouse and slept in a small room right off the engine bay.

THE BRUNSWICK VOLUNTEER FIRE COMPANY   1512
GENERAL FUND

BRUNSWICK, MD. April 23 1956   65-147
521

PAY TO THE ORDER OF American LaFrance Corporation. $ 39.38

Thirty Nine Dollars. And 38/00   DOLLARS

The Peoples National Bank
Brunswick, Maryland

THE BRUNSWICK VOLUNTEER FIRE COMPANY

by David F. Stickles
TREASURER

This is a check from the Brunswick Volunteer Fire Company from 1956. The check is made out to the American LaFrance Corporation. At that time, the company had four American LaFrance engines, a 1922, 1938, 1953, and a 1956. The company also had a 1930 Ford with a Howe body and pump.

This toy was a give-a-way during a fire prevention month in the 1970's/80's.

This photograph shows the 1971 GMC pumper parked in front of the old fire hall on West Potomac Street. The community anticipates the opening of a brewery in the old fire hall site.

Reader's Comments

Shortly after the release of Volume I, Charlie Smith identified himself as the man on the left in this photograph.

Correction

In Volume I, the author mistakenly stated that Sam Cincotta built the Cincotta building. In fact the building was constructed before Cincotta purchased the building.

Suggested Reading

Many time I am asked what books should be read about local history. Below are some books I suggest to readers who wish to learn more about the history of the area.

* Brunswick:100 Years of Memories, Brunswick History Commission

* Barry–Berlin–Brunswick, Dorthy Strathern

* Life in a Small Town 1880 to 1899, A Portrait of Knoxville, Maryland, Peter Maynard and Eleanor Milligan

* History In Our Attics: Photos and Documents of Brunswick, Maryland Volume I, James R. Castle

* Smith: Way Before We Were Brunswick, H.B. Funk

* Growing Up, Russell Baker

* History of Frederick County Maryland, T. J. C. Williams

I hope you enjoyed this book.

Coming in 2016:

History In Our Attics: Photos And Documents of Brunswick, Maryland

Volume III

More Railroad

Kaplon's Department Store

More Businesses

Sports

More School

Neighboring Communities

James R. Castle

P.O. Box 8

Brunswick, MD 21716

www.jamesrcastle.com

www.facebook.com/authorjamesrcastle

Email:jamesrcastle@comcast.net

46488265R00058

Made in the USA
Charleston, SC
21 September 2015